I CAN DRAW
DINOSAURS

BY LISA BONFORTE

A Little Simon Book
Published by Simon & Schuster, Inc., New York

Copyright © 1984 by Little Simon,
a Division of Simon & Schuster, Inc.
All rights reserved
including the right of reproduction
in whole or in part in any form
Published by LITTLE SIMON
A Division of Simon & Schuster, Inc.
Simon & Schuster Building
1230 Avenue of the Americas
New York, New York 10020
LITTLE SIMON and colophon are trademarks
of Simon & Schuster, Inc.
Manufactured in the United States of America

10 9 8

ISBN: 0-671-52756-8

BASIC BEGINNINGS

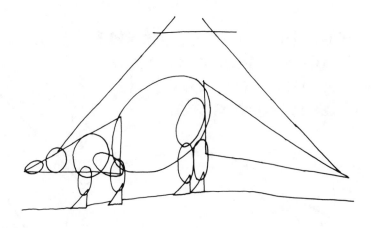

This is a book to show easy ways to draw dinosaurs. Squares, circles, ovals, rectangles and triangles are combined to make the basic form. The shapes are refined, step by step, until the drawing is complete. Details are then added for the finishing touches.

Naturally you will use different shapes as the underlying drawing for the different dinosaurs. With practice, it will become easy to recognize which shapes should be used to start each drawing.

If you are not happy with the way your drawings look, don't be afraid to draw them over until you like them.

Remember; practice makes perfect.

As an extra bonus this book has a put-together DINO-JAW you can assemble yourself.

BRONTOSAURUS

The Brontosaurus is made up of the same simple basic shapes that you will use for every dinosaur in this book. Draw the shapes together as they are here.

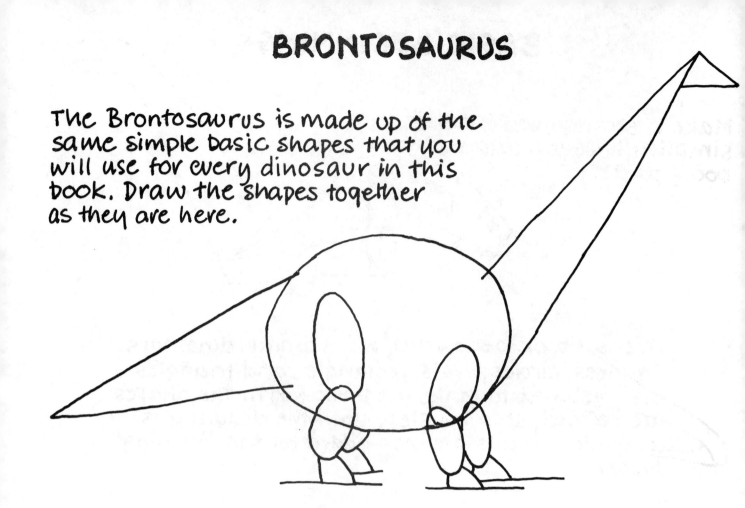

Over the basic shapes, add smooth lines to make the simple outline.

Make a strong exterior line and simplify lines for legs and other body parts.

Erase guidelines and add features like toes, eyes, nostrils and skin folds.

BRONTOSAURUS 3/4 VIEW

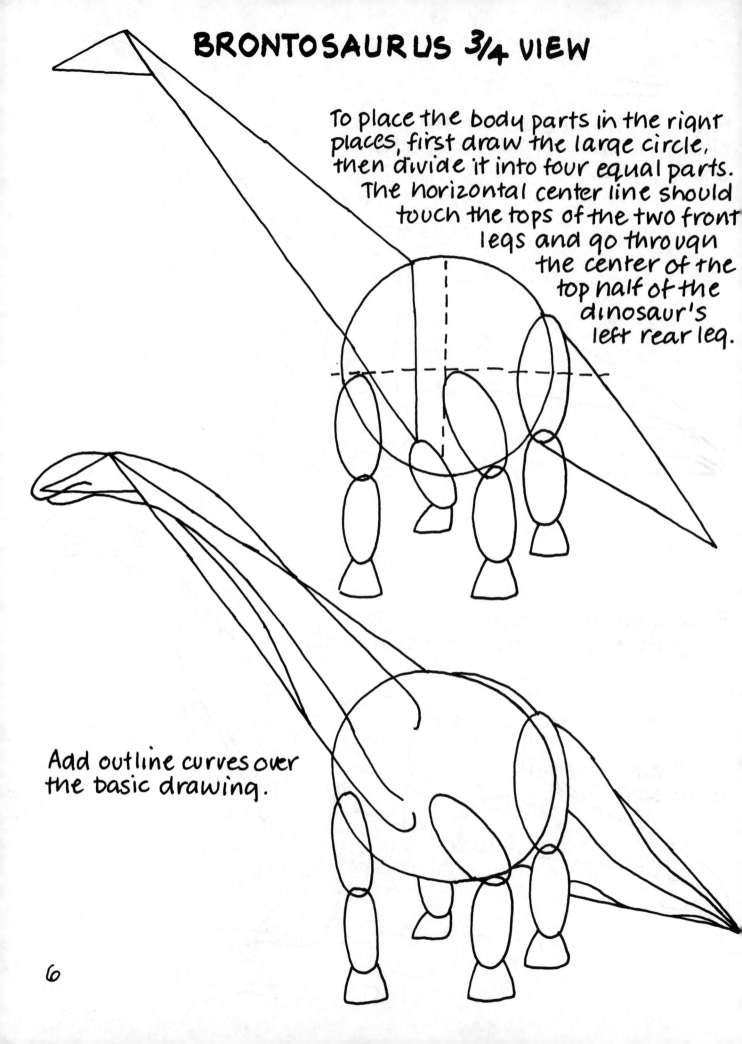

To place the body parts in the right places, first draw the large circle, then divide it into four equal parts. The horizontal center line should touch the tops of the two front legs and go through the center of the top half of the dinosaur's left rear leg.

Add outline curves over the basic drawing.

Erase guidelines.

Add eyes, nostrils, toes
and skin folds.

7

STEGOSAURUS

Use triangles, ovals and circles to form the body.

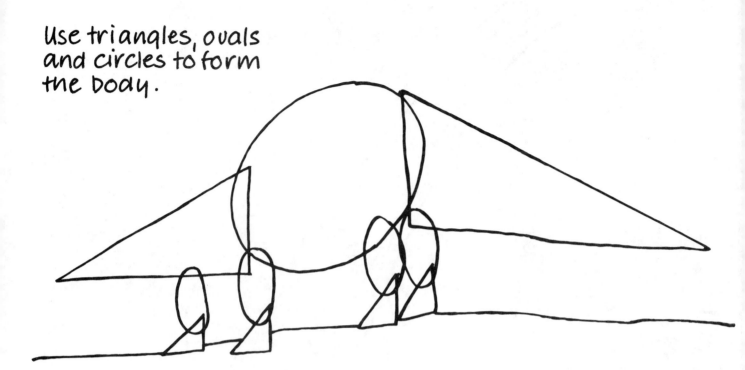

Add more body features with basic shapes within and around the larger shapes.

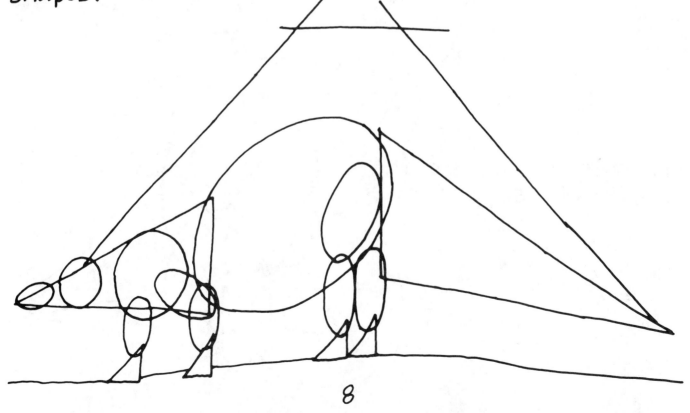

Draw diamond shapes to create back blades. Outline curves are added.

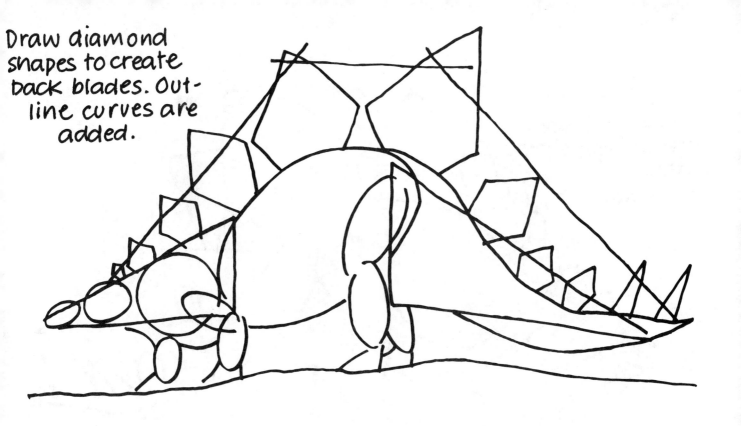

Add a second row of back blades and toes and erase unnecessary guidelines

Finish erasing guidelines
and add features
such as eye, mouth,
nostril and
skin folds.

Complete all details and add shading to give
the creature a life-like appearance.

TRICERATOPS

Start with three simple shapes—a circle and two incomplete triangles. Do not draw the dotted lines.

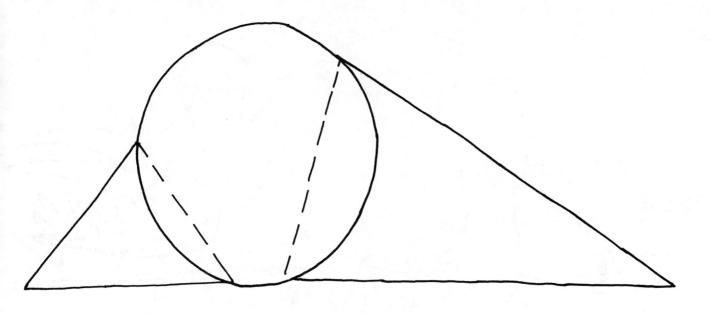

Add legs, feet, head and horns as shown.

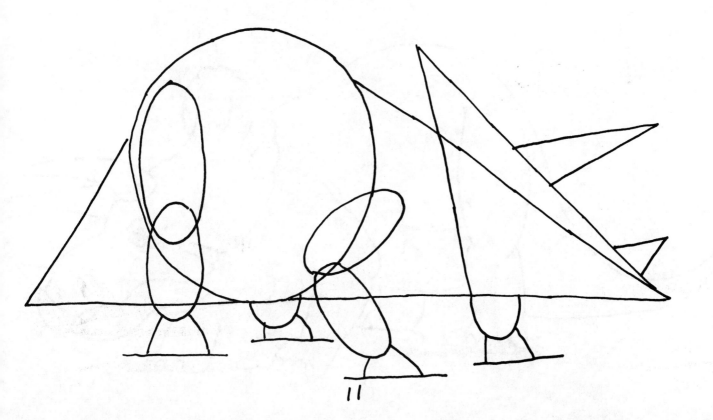

Make a dark outline, along with curves for the legs and head. Finish horns and add an eye.

Complete the head, eye, toes and other features.

TRICERATOPS AND HIS SKULL

Now that you know how to draw this dinosaur you can have some fun seeing what lies beneath the skin of his head.

On tracing paper, trace the head and place it over the picture of the Triceratops' skull.

PTERANODON

Draw the simple shapes.
Notice curved line for the
left wing and the V-shaped
mouth.

Add other curved lines, eye, nostril, wing
claws and feet.

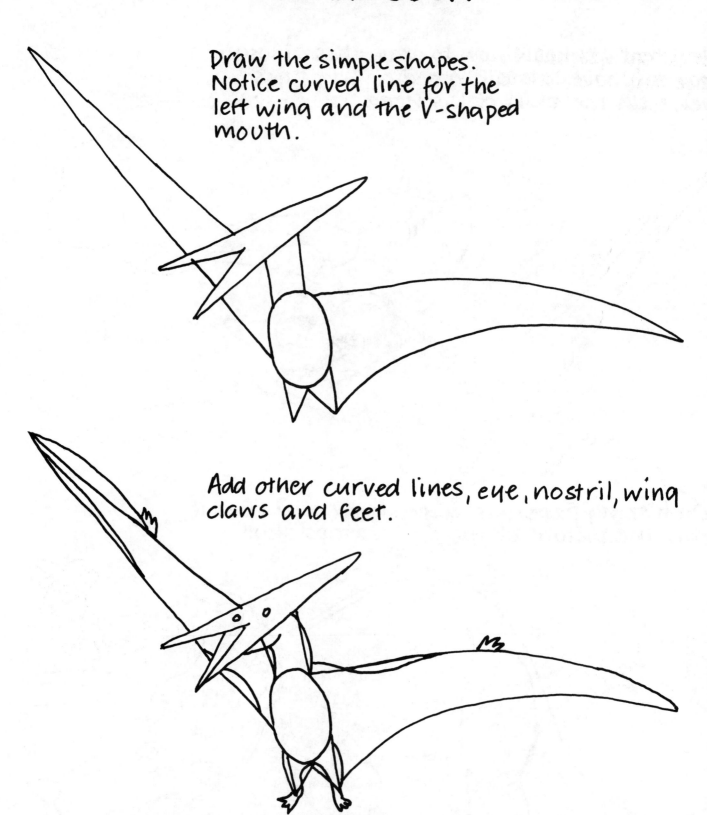

Erase guidelines. Finish
eye and wing details.

STYRAKOSAURUS

The first step for the Styrakosaurus is almost the same as with the Triceratops, but here you use an oval instead of a circle.

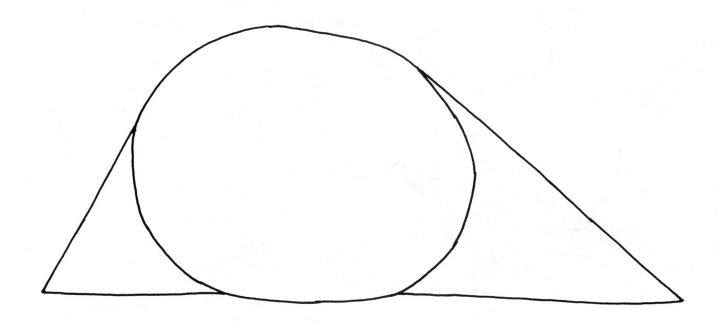

Add legs and head as shown.

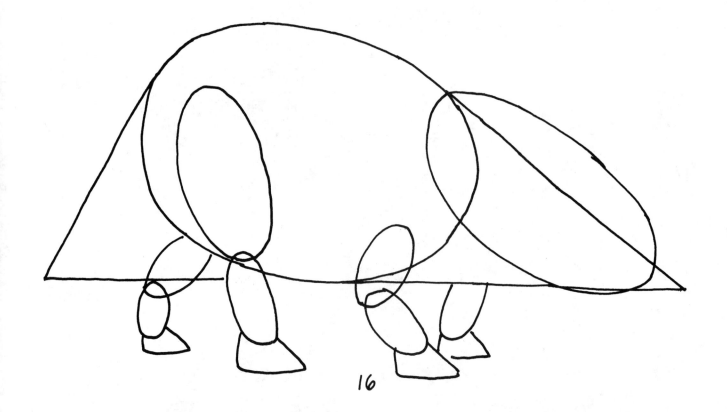

Smooth the outlines for the legs and tail. Add two over-
lapping ovals for the head. Make horns, some smaller
ones and some larger ones, as shown. Place the eye in
the center where the two ovals overlap. Add nose horn.

Finish by outlining the head and adding the beak, toes,
nostril and skin folds.

17

CORYTHOSAURUS SKULL

This is a picture of the Corythosaurus skull.

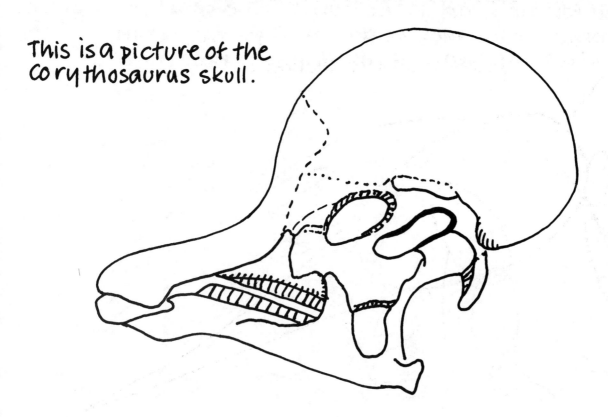

Trace the Corythosaurus head, and place the tracing over the skull.

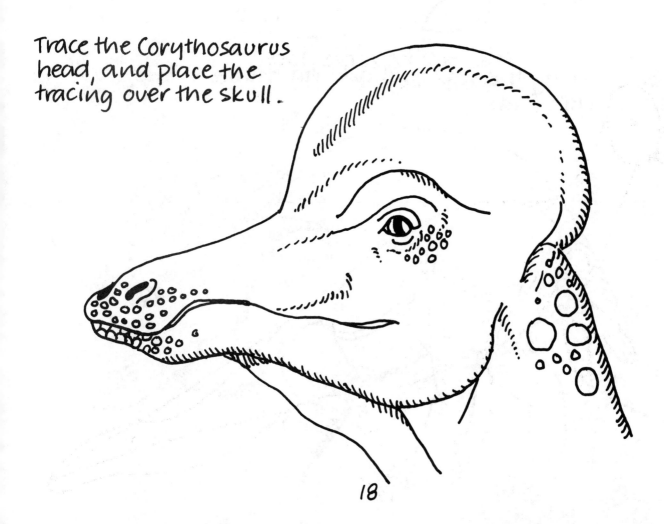

CORYTHOSAURUS

Draw the basic shapes.

Add outline curve, toes,
nostril and eye.

19

Erase unnecessary guidelines.
Define fingers and toes and
add some details.

Finish the details. See this page
and the next page for more
close-up details.

CORYTHOSAURUS CLOSE UP

Notice his scaley skin. He had webbing between his four fingers and knuckles in the middle of each finger.

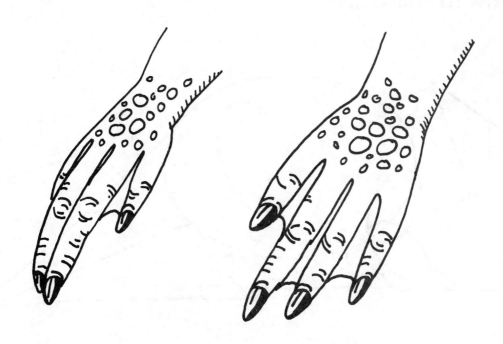

His feet had three toes, with claw-like toenails, and many wrinkle lines on each toe.

Don't forget to add all details to your own drawing.

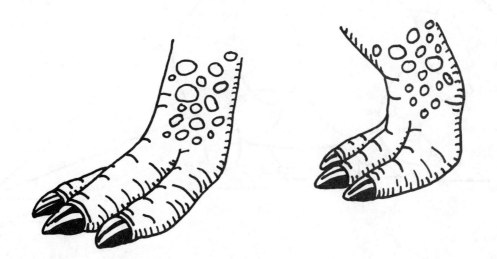

PROTOCERATOPS

Make the simple shapes. The tail of the Protoceratops touched the ground when he stood, so make it touch the same ground line as the legs closest to you. Notice his legs are bent at the knees.

Add curves for his head, and give him an eye.

Make outline curves, mouth and beak. Erase all unnecessary guidelines.

Finish by adding details.

PARASAUROLOPHUS SKULL AND HEAD

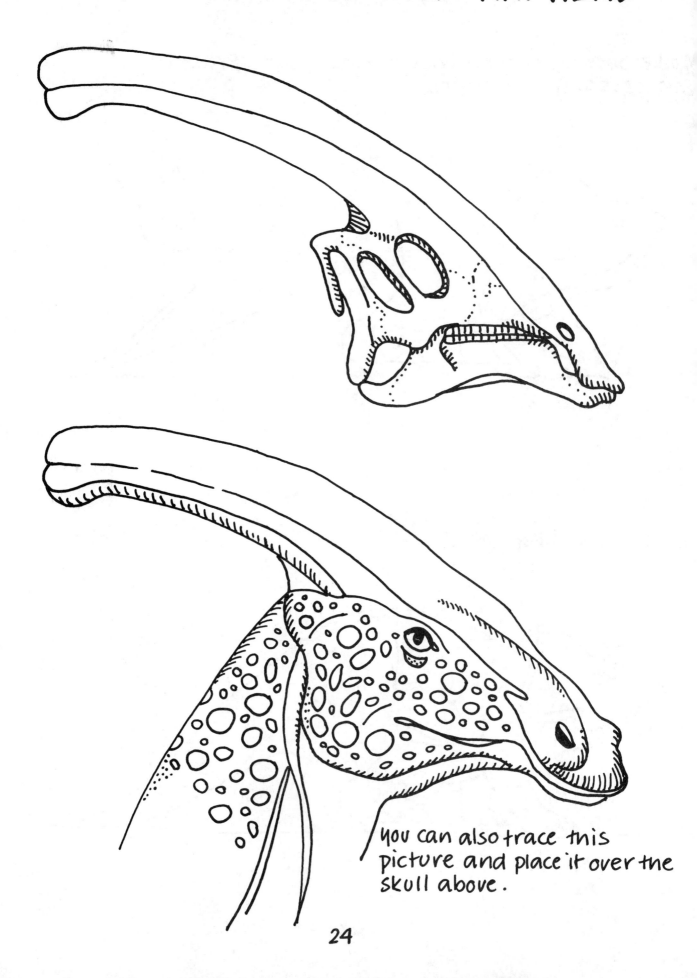

You can also trace this picture and place it over the skull above.

PARASAUROLOPHUS

Draw shapes as shown. The tail touched the ground so put in a ground line with the leg closest to you.

Add body curves.

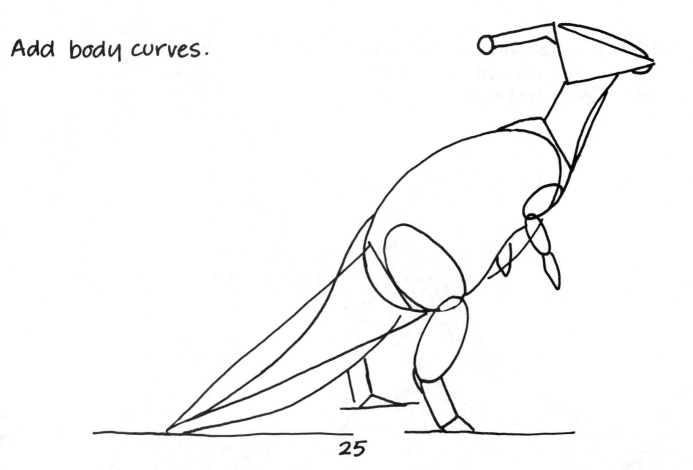

Erase unneeded guidelines and add fingers and toes.

Add all finishing features and details – many are like those on the Corythosaurus.

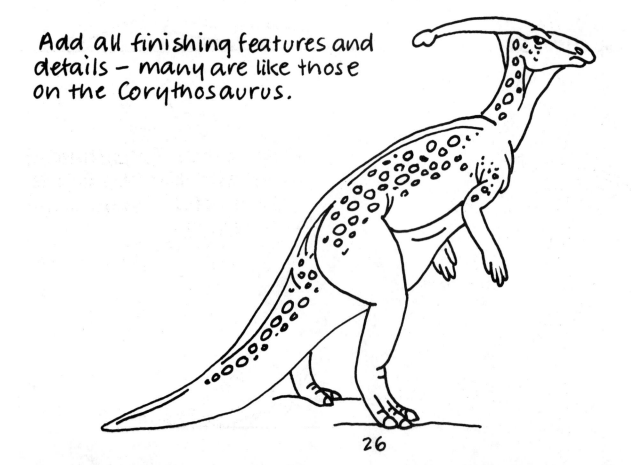

IGUANODON

Draw shapes and ground line.

Add curves for outline of head and tail. Put in the eye, nostril, fingers, and toes.

Erase guidelines and start
to add details.

Finish features and details.

28

IGUANODON DETAILS

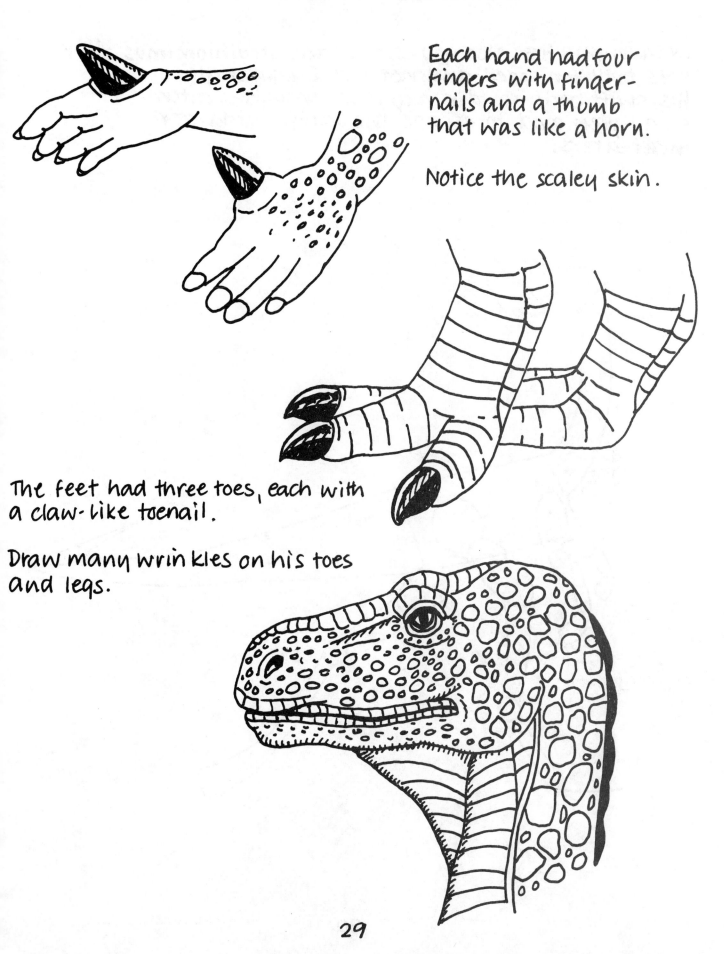

Each hand had four fingers with finger-nails and a thumb that was like a horn.

Notice the scaley skin.

The feet had three toes, each with a claw-like toenail.

Draw many wrinkles on his toes and legs.

STRUTHIOMIMUS "OSTRICH MIMIC"

Even in this first step you can see the Struthiomimus was built for speed and not just for strength. His swift body could run quickly enough to catch small prey and to escape the danger of larger meat-eaters.

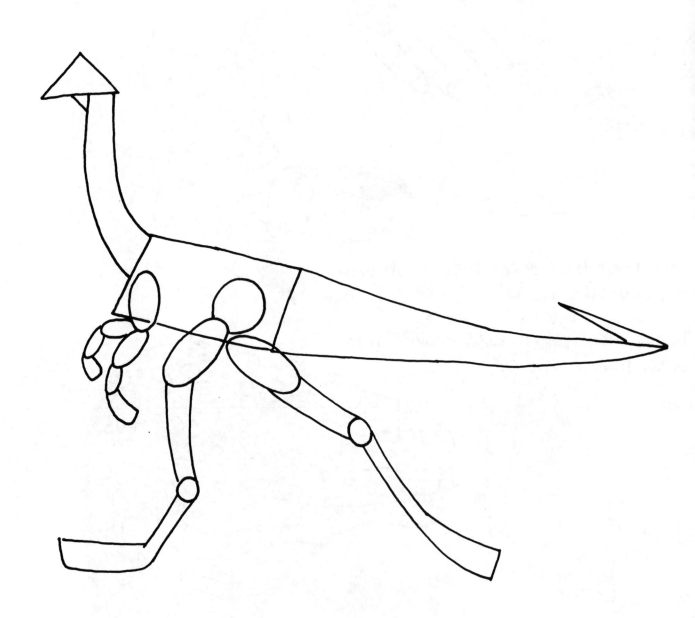

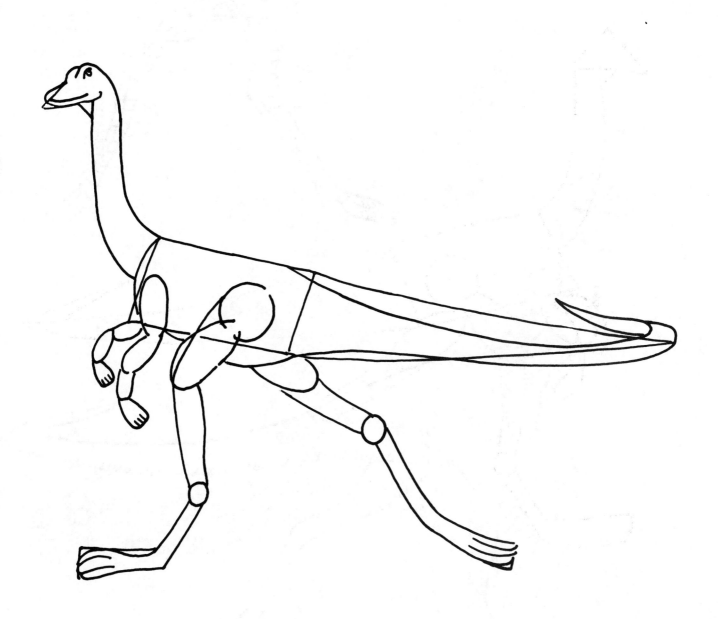

It is easy to see where the Struthiomimus (ostrich mimic) got its name. The dinosaur was even about the same size as an ostrich is today.

HADROSAURUS THE "DUCKBILL"

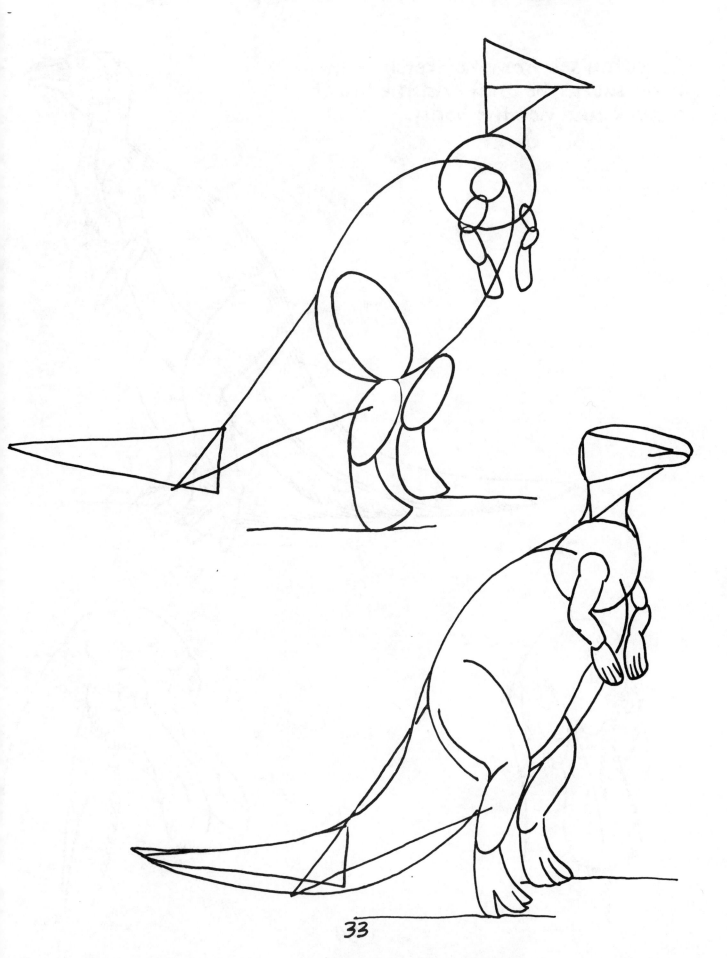

As you can see from the sketch of the Hadrosaurus, he only had the bill of a duck and not the body.

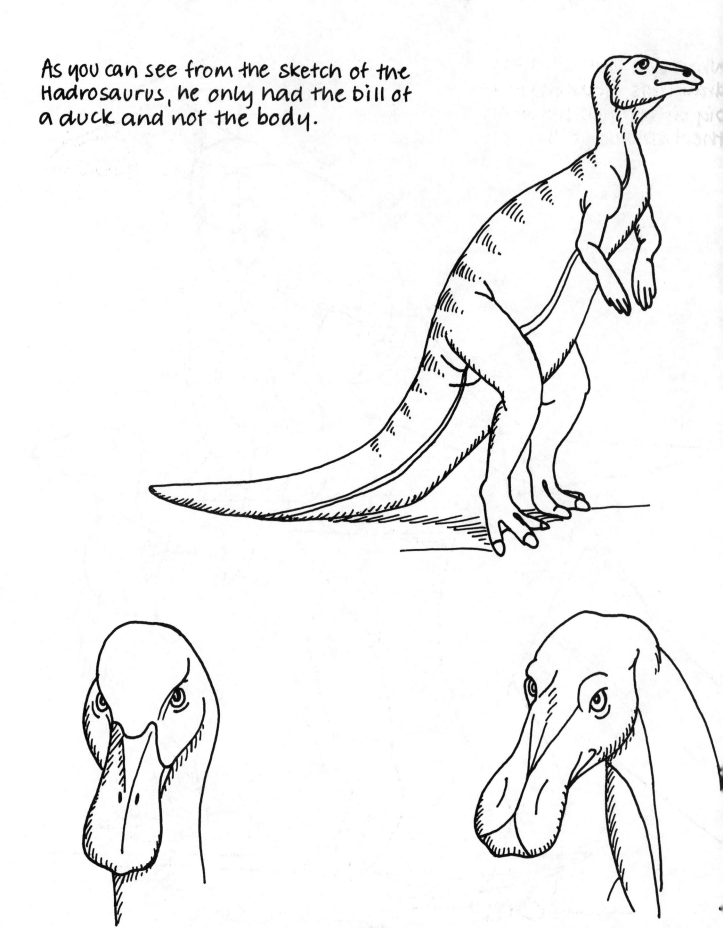

HADROSAURUS AND DUCK

When you look at these drawings, you can see a big difference between the two duckbills.

HADROSAURUS

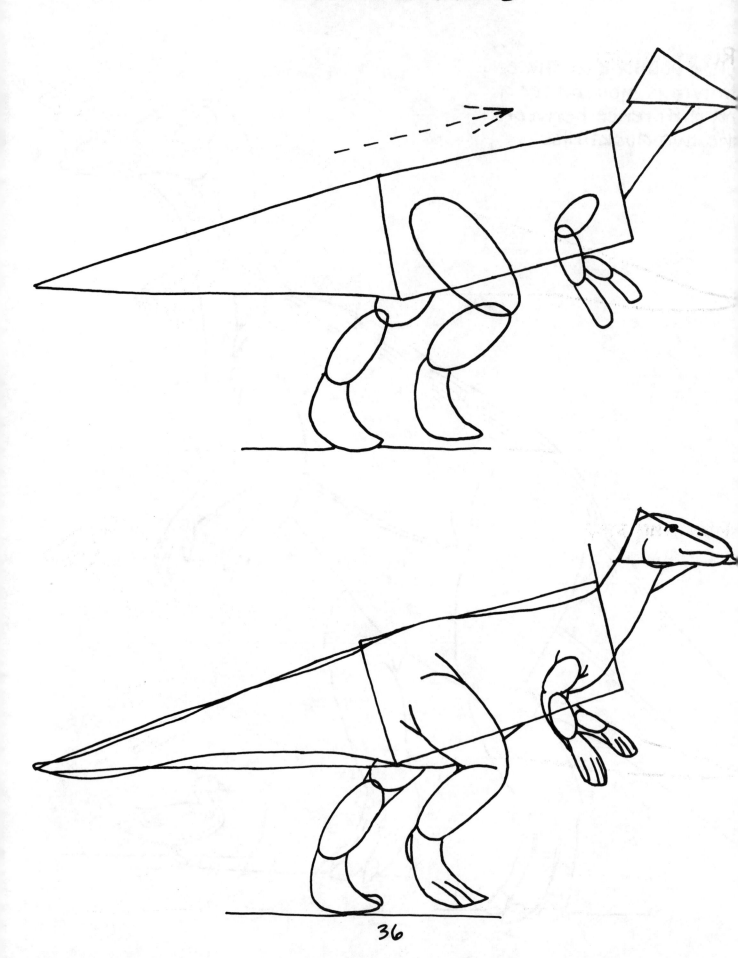

Running step

Walking step

Sizes of various dinosaurs compared with
animals of today.

TYRANNOSAURUS REX

Head and skull details

Notice the mighty jaw with its large teeth. This was the Tyrannosaurus' defense weapon against all dinosaurs

TYRANNOSAURUS SKELETON

This is the entire skeleton of a Tyrannosaurus. Even underneath his skin and muscles you can see he was a powerful animal.

Notice his large head and jaws and the sturdy legs that were used to carry his huge body. His tail also had to be heavy and strong to balance all the weight his legs had to carry.

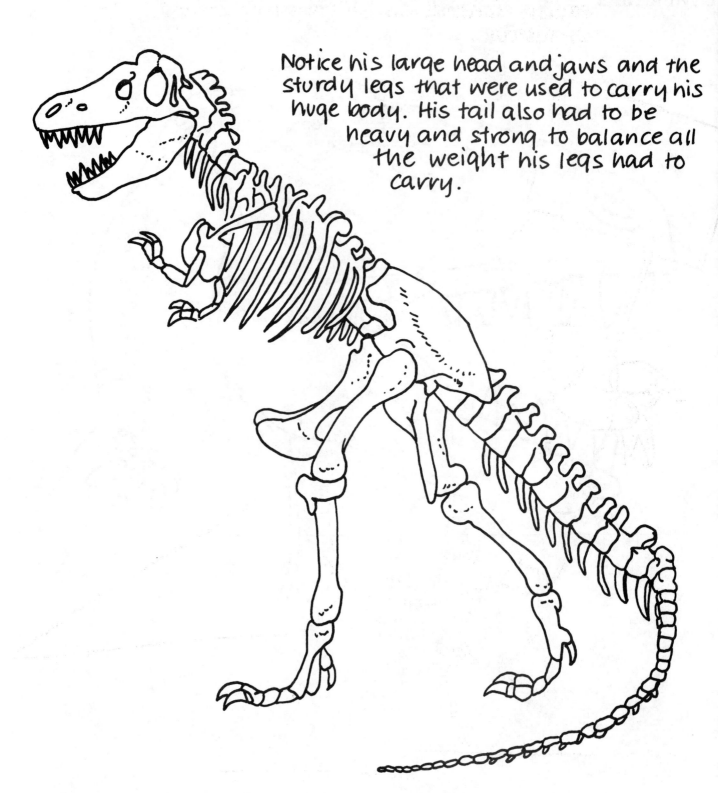

TYRANNOSAURUS

By looking at this simple drawing you can see that the Tyrannosaurus could easily defend himself against other dinosaurs.

Add the eye, nostril, mouth and claws on the feet.

Smooth the outlines of the legs, arms and head. Don't forget to add the tip of his tail

Simplify your drawing by erasing all unnecessary guidelines.

As in all the other drawings, add finishing features to complete your Tyrannosaurus.

NANOSAURUS

You have already seen how massive dinosaurs could be when you drew the
Brontosaurus. Now take a look at the Nanosaurus.
He was only as big as a wild turkey is today.

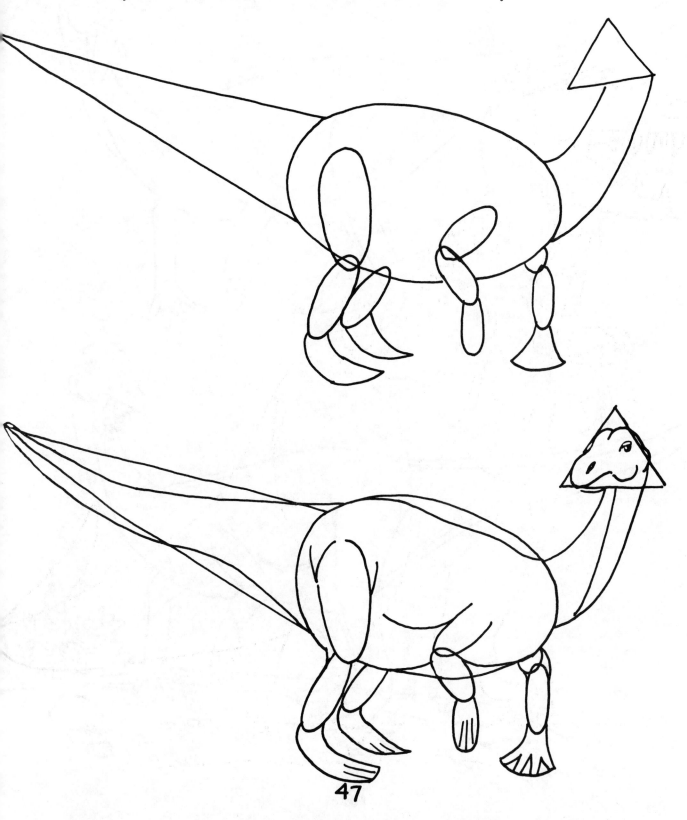

47

A hungry Nanosaurus looks and listens as he eats his meal. He was always on the lookout for larger dinosaurs who may have wanted to eat <u>him</u> for lunch.

48

SALTOPUS

Draw the simple shapes.

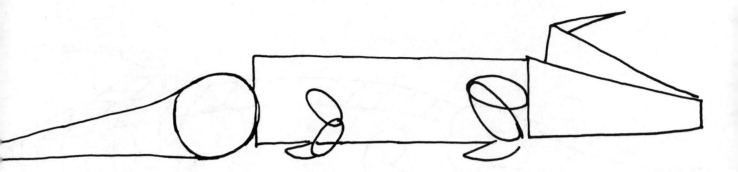

Add curves for the outline.

Erase all unnecessary guidelines and start adding features as shown.

Add eye, nostril, toes, scales and teeth to complete your drawing of the Saltopus.

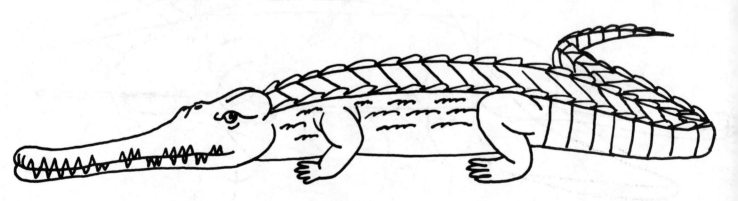

50

TRICERATOPS COMING AND GOING

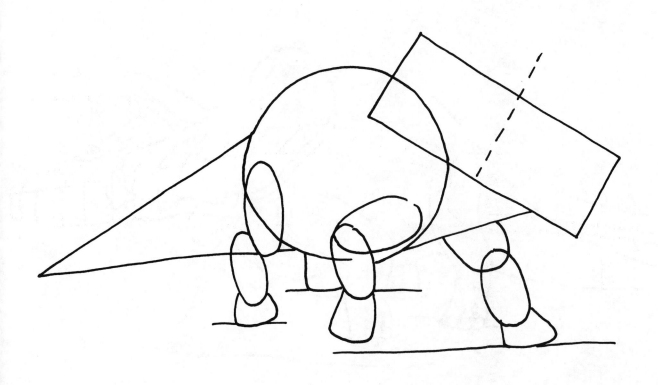

COMING

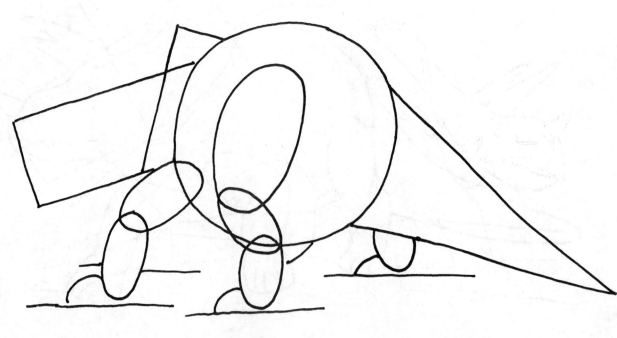

GOING

PROTECTION

Different body parts that protected the dinosaurs.

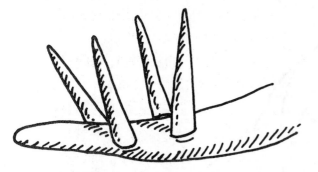

Spiked Stregasaurus tail

Strong jaw and sharp teeth of Tyrannosaurus.

Horn, beak and helmet-like crest of Triceratops.

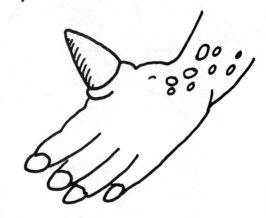

Spiked Iguanodon thumb.

Horn, beak and spiked crest of the Styracosaurus.

DRAWING A LANDSCAPE

For step one draw a horizon line. Next pick a point on the horizon line (this point is called the vanishing point). Now draw a line from the tip of the dinosaur's head to the vanishing point, then one from his foot to the same point.

Draw a smaller dinosaur closer to the vanishing point with the lines touching his head and feet, as with the first dinosaur. The two dinosaurs are the same size but, since one is farther away, he looks smaller. This is perspective.

In step two erase your perspective lines, add a mountain range, some clouds in the sky and a volcano with smoke.

To help complete your landscape, add hills in front of the mountain range, and some trees, plants and a pond in the foreground.

IN AIR AND ON LAND

While some dinosaurs like the Brachiosaurus seemed to be able to touch the sky, others, like the Pteranodon, could actually fly.

THE BATTLE

FAMILY GROUP

This dinosaur mom kept a close watch over her noisy little babies as they played in their nest made from a mound of dirt.

60

PROTOCERATOPS

Like many other dinosaurs, the Protoceratops hatched from eggs buried in a nest of sand. The Protoceratops mother stayed near the nest to protect and raise her children

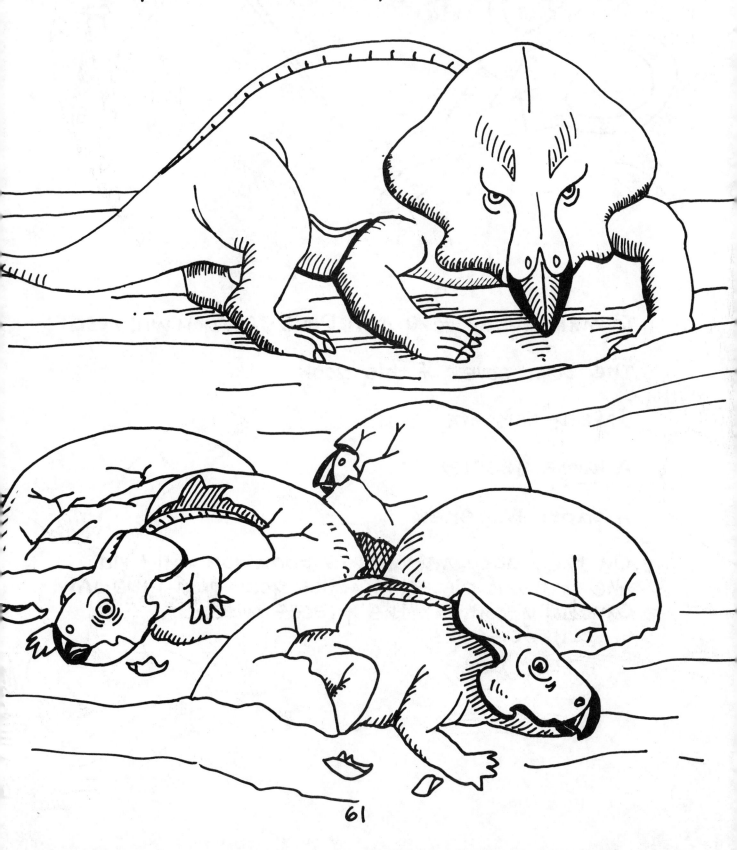

ASSEMBLING

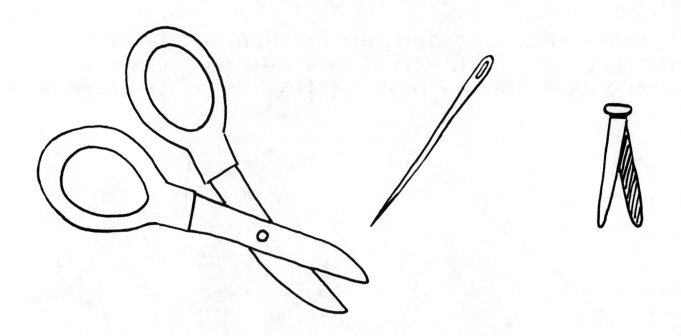

1. To make your very own DINO-JAW you will need:

   The back cover of this book

   Safety scissors

   A large needle

   A paper fastener

2. On the back cover of this book you will find the pattern pieces to make your own DINO-JAW. Carefully cut out the pieces with safety scissors.

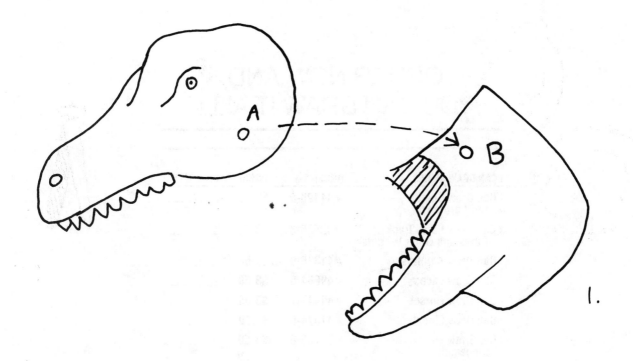

1.

3. Puncture through the dots marked A and B.
   Be very careful not to hurt yourself.

4. Place A over B as shown in diagram 1 and 2.

5. Use the paper fastener to join the pieces together.

Have fun!

2.

ORDER NOW AND
YOU CAN DRAW IT ALL!

I CAN DRAW SERIES	ORDER NO.	PRICE	QUANTITY
I Can Draw Comics and Cartoons	#44490-5	$2.95	_____
I Can Draw Cars, Trucks, Trains and Other Wheels	#42535-8	$3.50	_____
I Can Draw Animals	#41375-9	$3.50	_____
I Can Draw Faces	#49664-6	$3.50	_____
I Can Draw Horses	#46447-7	$3.50	_____
I Can Draw Monsters	#41374-0	$3.50	_____
I Can Draw Dinosaurs	#52756-8	$3.50	_____
The Giant I Can Draw Everything	#44459-X	$4.95	_____

NO RISK OFFER · RETURN THIS COUPON TODAY!

Simon & Schuster, Inc.
1230 Avenue of the Americas · New York, N.Y. 10020
Attn: Mail Order Dept. ICD4

Please send me copies of the books checked. (If not completely satisfied, return for full refund within 14 days.)

Enclose full amount per copy with this coupon. (Send check or money order only.)

Please be sure to include proper postage and handling:
95¢—first copy
50¢—each additional copy ordered

If order is for $10.00 or more, you may charge to one of the following accounts:
MasterCard   Visa

Name_____

Address_____

City_____

State_____Zip Code_____

Credit Card No._____

Card Expiration Date_____

Signature_____

Books listed are also available at your local bookstore. Prices are subject to change without notice.